HAP

It's l

My goal is to inspire you to get back to the basics of happy living so that you can enjoy a more fulfilling life and not feel overwhelmed by the complexities of society at the turn of the millennium.

Together we will explore the insights offered by a fun and creative interaction with seven ordinary items:

- Penny
- Hershey's Kiss*
- Elastic Band
- Pencil
- Crayon
- Candle
- Seashell

These simple items symbolize fundamental principles for joyful, balanced living. Activities at the end of each chapter provide practical ways you can incorporate each basic concept into your daily life.

Insights into communication, perspective, positive thinking, faith, creativity, humor—these are just a few of the many morsels of wisdom that await you.

Enjoy!

—Dianne Durante

To my two role models:

My mother, **Ami Durante,**
Who gave me the greatest gift
—LIFE—
And then showed me how to live
With love, dedication, and hard work;

And my daughter, **Kirsten Hagman,**
Who gave me the greatest reason for living
—LOVE—
And challenges me to live a life of freedom and passion.
You're the best!

And to the memory of my Dad, **Leo,**
The wind beneath my wings, who guides me from heaven
With his laughter and saxophone.

—D.D.

My Bag of Gratitude and Appreciation

A pencil, eraser, and elastic band to **Lane Hawley Cole.** Eight years ago I began my "It's In The Bag" lecture. For two years, I struggled to write this book, spinning my wheels and not making much progress. Then I found Lane. She has been my pencil, eraser, and elastic band—encouraging me, questioning me, re-writing, and reviewing. She has helped me to stretch myself without snapping and to find ways to keep the book clear and simple.

A bag full of pennies to my cousin and best friend, **Judy Kemble.** Judy is not only my business partner and publicist, but also my left and right arm. She provides daily encouragement and applies her management and organizational skills as we chart our path.

A bag full of chocolate kisses to my dear friends and colleagues, **Pam Zabitchuck** and **Carolyn Ryan.** Pam used her genius computer skills to create the prototype reminder cards and has spent incalculable time researching, proof-reading, and brainstorming. Most importantly, she's the one who found Karla Wheeler. Pam continues to be part of the team, working tirelessly to make this project a success. Carolyn encouraged me more than two years ago to put my thoughts on paper and create this book. She typed and retyped the first draft and continues to provide unending support.

Many pennies go to all those who have read the manuscript and shared their thoughts: **Stella Papalos, Nancy Fitzgerald, June Davis, Ann Wydman, Maxine Dziedric, Hazel Achor, Lillian Zabitchuck, Mark Merenda, Lou Traina, Bobby Roth, Jeff Moses, Marci Shimoff, Patty Aubrey, Jack Canfield,** and **Harold Bloomfield.**

A candle to my sister, **Joyce Durante,** who flies from New York to Rome just to make me laugh and play.

Seashells to **my clients** who have shared their vulnerabilities.

A huge box of crayons to cover designer **Helen Suydam Ruisi,** who captured the joyful essence of the book so magnificently.

A brightly colored crayon to graphic artists **Mike Morse, Denyce Rusch,** and **Gayle Stan.**

Finally, my heartfelt thanks to book producers **Universal Life Matters, Inc.,** whose founders make this seem like a playful journey. To **Jan Doetsch,** who dotted all the i's and crossed all the t's so joyfully and skillfully. To **Joyceanna Rautio,** whose professional and strategic plan was always there. And to **Karla Wheeler,** editor and designer extraordinaire, whose heart energy, enthusiasm, and belief in my dream have made it the reality you hold in your hand today. She was sent by the angels to me.

—Dianne Durante

Contents

Symbol Six: A CANDLE

127

Symbol Seven: A SEASHELL

147

Closing: YOUR LUNCH BAG TO GO

167

A Bag of Basic Ingredients

A Bag of
Basic Ingredients

Many years ago, my mother gave me her eighth-grade cookbook, *The Preparation of Food*. Published in 1922, the small, plain, brown book was used by the Chicago public schools to teach young women how to feed, nurture, and be good caretakers of the family.

It was a "how-to" book of its day: how to prepare food and plan family meals. It presented things plainly and very clearly—a no-frills book. But then, maybe those were no-frills days: "Just the facts, ma'am," as Joe Friday of *Dragnet* would say, "nothing but the facts."

My mom's cookbook taught the basics of food preparation. This brown-bag book presents seven basic, ordinary items that have extraordinary significance for a happy life. *HAPPINESS: It's In the Bag!* is packed with little morsels of wisdom.

I have been using this wisdom for the last 20 years in my practice as a marriage and family therapist. I was trained in the New York/New Jersey area by some of the masters in the field of family therapy, and I learned the most advanced techniques. But I've observed that advanced techniques and theories can obscure the fact that there are fundamental principles involved in every healthy human interaction. These basics for a rewarding life are very much the same today as they were in the old days—just as the basic ingredients for biscuits in my mother's cookbook still make mouthwatering biscuits today.

I have been giving workshops on this topic for years, calling my lecture "It's in the Bag." Everyone who attends the workshop receives a small brown bag (your basic lunch bag) containing common items used as symbols for a healthy life.

Before you begin the following chapters, I would like you to take a walk around your house. Go on a scavenger hunt for the following basic items: a brown lunch bag, a penny, a Hershey's kiss, an elastic band, a pencil with an eraser, a crayon, a birthday candle, and a seashell (if you don't live by the sea, just improvise). Or, if you prefer, you may just cut out and use the "reminder cards," which you'll find in the back of the book.

Now sit back and get ready for your hands-on workshop. The more senses you involve in your learning process, the more likely it is that you will remember the information and use it in your life, and the more enjoyable that process will be. Thus, I have suggested some workbook activities at the end of each section to help you incorporate these basic concepts into your behavior.

My hope is that you will also tap into a level of personal meaning for the symbols. For that reason, I have left space at the end of each chapter for you to add your own perceptions and creative connections to the symbols.

SYMBOL ONE

A Penny

HAPPINESS: It's In The Bag!

Chapter 1

A Penny for Your Thoughts

Communication

The first symbol in the bag is a penny. What does the penny remind you of? Suggestion: "A penny for your thoughts." This old saying focuses on the importance of *communication*, sharing our thoughts and ideas with others. When we share, a listener needs to be present as well as a speaker. How often in our daily lives do we see people rattling off their thoughts, always talking, but no one is listening. Stephen King's short story "The Body" has a wonderful prologue:

> The most important things are the hardest things to say. They are the things you get ashamed of, because words diminish them—words shrink things that seemed limitless when they were in your head to no more than living size when they're brought out. But it's more than that, isn't it? The most important things lie too close to wherever your secret heart is buried, like landmarks to a treasure your enemies would love to steal away. And you may make revelations that cost you dearly only to have people look at

you in a funny way, not understanding what you've said at all, or why you thought it was so important that you almost cried while you were saying it. That's the worst, I think. When the secret stays locked within not for want of a teller but for want of an understanding ear.

Imagine the secrets that stay locked within us because we cannot find some-one to open their ears and hearts to hear us. "To **hear**(t) with the **heart** and the (h)**ear**(t) is an (he)**art**." —*Cliff Durfee.*

In fact, in our society we probably spend too much time teaching speaking skills and not nearly enough time teaching listening skills.

And do we remember to listen to ourselves? A penny for your thoughts and my thoughts, too. How important it is to pay attention to our-selves. When we value what we say to ourselves, others will value what we say to them.

> *The first duty of love is to listen.*
>
> — *Paul Tillich*

When you talk to yourself, talk in positive terms. Encourage yourself. Pat yourself on the back for a job well done. Pay extra attention to what you say to yourself in times of distress or ad-versity.

One final word on communication. Often in therapy when couples come in, one partner will say, "I shouldn't have to tell her what I want, we've been together for nine years, she should know." Get serious! No one is a mind reader. We need to take responsibility for ourselves and ask for what we need. Communicate it clearly. We also need to ask the other person what they need from us. So often in relationships, listening and being present are tough. Asking takes courage and trust. So be brave—just ask!

"A penny for your thoughts" reminds us to communicate clearly.

HAPPINESS: It's In The Bag!

ACTIVITIES FOR ENHANCING COMMUNICATION

1. You have two ears and one mouth. Use them in that ratio.

   a) Pick a day (Monday) and practice listening. Imagine you have laryngitis and can't talk. Listen for one day without talking.

   b) Actively listen, repeat what people say, and then state your comment.

   Example: Tom says, "What a terrible day at work!" Mary says, "Sounds like you really had an awful day. Do you want to talk about it?" Then she listens. Later, Mary asks Tom for a few minutes to share her thoughts.

2. Your body language can "speak" with more impact than your words.

   Imagine you are on TV and watch yourself as you talk to others. Notice your facial expression, where your arms are, your eye contact. "I love you" said with your arms crossed is a lot different from "I love you" said in an embrace, looking deeply into your loved one's eyes.

   Communication is:

   > 56% body language
   > 36% tone
   > *8% actual words!*

---

3. Pay attention to the three levels of communication:

   a) What you mean to say

   b) How you say it—tone and body language

   c) How the listener interprets what you have said

4. Learn and use "I messages." An "I message" is a simple, clear, and effective form of communication, especially when you have strong feelings about an issue.

   An example of an "I message" is: "When you (describe action), I feel (state your feeling), because (how action affects you). What I need from you is (describe behavior you want from person)." This helps the communicator clearly describe the offensive behavior and *accept her feelings* as a result of the behavior.

   Example: "When you are late for dinner, I feel scared, because I am afraid you may have gotten into an accident. What I need is for you to call if you will be more than 30 minutes late."

NOTES

_____

_____

_____

_____

_____

_____

_____

_____

_____

_____

_____

_____

_____

_____

_____

_____

_____

_____

_____

_____

NOTES

_____

_____

_____

_____

_____

_____

_____

_____

_____

_____

_____

_____

_____

_____

_____

_____

HAPPINESS: It's In The Bag!

Chapter 2

A Penny
Two Sides

A few years ago I was teaching a college sociology course called "Love and Relationships." I reached into my bag and pulled out a penny, then invited suggestions from the class on how this penny could symbolize something we needed in life. One of the students suggested, "A penny has two sides, and you need to remember to look at both sides." How true.

> *The best way to have a good idea is to have lots of ideas.*
>
> — Linus Pauling

> *Minds are like parachutes. They only function when open.*
>
> — Sark

Actually, we need to remember to look at *numerous* sides or ways to address issues in our lives. Brainstorm! Be creative. Explore many dimensions to find a resolution to your problems. Expand your vision. Call in experts if need be. Talk to friends. Think of what your enemies would do. Take in as much information as you can.

> *Great spirit, grant that I may not criticize my neighbor until I have walked a mile in his moccasins.*
>
> *— Native American Saying*

Broaden your vision.

It's healthy to try to look from another's direction. It reminds us that people see the world as *they* are, wearing gray, amber, or rose-colored glasses. We set ourselves free of judgmental behavior when we choose a vision that respects differences. Everyone wins when we accept one another's rights to freedom of choice.

Remember, the penny has two sides, and each side is as valid and valuable as the other.

ACTIVITIES FOR SEEING DIFFERENT SIDES

1. Agree to disagree.

   The next time you are in a heated conflict with someone, call a "time out" and say, "I guess we need to agree to disagree." This creates a win-win situation rather than a win-lose event. If a decision needs to be made, flip a coin (penny) and whoever wins gets their way. Or you could solve conflicts by choosing even/odd days. Monday, Wednesday, Friday—it's your way. Tuesday, Thursday, Saturday—it's mine. This works great for minor family feuds.

   Caveat: This method may *not* be appropriate for major decisions: "OK it's Monday. I get to have a baby whether you want one now or not."

2. Walk a mile in their moccasins or wingtips.

   a) If you're alone:

   To view life from another perspective, imagine you *are* the other person. Stand or sit the way they do. Try to debate the issue from their viewpoint. Try to see and understand the issue from their perspective, with their background of experiences.

b) If you're with a friend:

You need a half-hour for this activity. Follow your friend (literally) on a street, shopping, or in nature. Walk behind and mirror them. Notice their breathing, their body motion or openness and try to copy it. Then switch roles. Each person follows for 10 minutes and then talks about what they've discovered.

3. Brainstorm.

Sit with a group (more than one). Name the issue or problem you are exploring. List all of the ways this issue could be looked at, no matter how crazy or ridiculous. Let one idea lead you to another. Keep it flowing, and write down everything.

Example: Problem—broke, in debt, need money.

I could: move to another state where there are more jobs, borrow from my family, borrow against my house, cut my expenses and have a roommate, enter a credit-counseling program, declare bankruptcy, sell my possessions and start over, work two jobs, go back to school, win the lottery, or start a home business.

No censoring or comments at this point, just list everything that comes to mind. After you have explored all the options and made your list of all the sides, begin filtering out the one(s) you want to try, then try them.

NOTES

_____

_____

_____

_____

_____

_____

_____

_____

_____

_____

_____

_____

_____

_____

_____

_____

_____

NOTES

_____

_____

_____

_____

_____

_____

_____

_____

_____

_____

_____

_____

_____

_____

_____

_____

_____

Chapter 3

A Penny
More Than Luck

"Find a penny, pick it up. All the day you'll have good luck." What is luck? Luck, according to *Webster's 9th New Collegiate Dictionary*, is "the ability to prosper or succeed, especially through chance or good for-

> *If you think you can, or you think you can't, you're right.*
> — *Henry Ford*

tune." Yet, if I believe I am lucky I will act very differently from the way that I would if I think I am unlucky. It really is a mindset, a way of thinking, believing, and acting, that creates one's reality.

So, this lucky penny can represent the need to *think positively*. Our society has a difficult time with this con- cept. From our earliest years, we are taught to think, "What's wrong with me?" not, "What's right?" In school, teachers check off all the errors with red ink, rather than putting "C" for "correct" on all the answers that are right.

If we truly wanted to change and grow, we would focus much more on the

---

positive. We would look for the healthy aspects of ourselves and others, rather than the unhealthy qualities. We would watch our language, and speak only in positive ways to others as well as to ourselves. We would use uplifting words to describe or label, words like "beautiful, smart, happy," rather than destructive words such as "ugly, stupid, lazy." Uplifting words create a peaceful environment. Labels stick. Perhaps some of us have said, "Sticks and stones may break my bones,

> *If you judge people, you have no time to love them.*
> — *Mother Teresa*

but words will never hurt me," and suffered in silence from unkind words. Words *do* hurt. They break our spirits, not our bones.

> *There are only two ways to live your life. One is as though nothing is a miracle, the other is as though everything is a miracle.*
> — *Albert Einstein*

There has been research on relationships suggesting that for every negative comment, we need five positive comments to create a healthy balance. Often when I have families in for therapy, each family member gets a chance to sit in the "honored person" spot and receive honor, respect, and praise for a few minutes. One can almost see this person growing an inch taller. The honored person must just listen and accept the positive comments, which is not an easy task. Family members rarely hear such praise and find it difficult at first to accept. However, everyone agrees that the positive feedback feels great.

Let the penny remind you to be positive and to see the miracles in everyday life.

ACTIVITIES FOR DEVELOPING
AN "I CAN" ATTITUDE

1. Spend a day without denouncing anyone or speaking negatively.

   If we spoke to our friends as we do to our family, we'd have no friends. This Sunday, practice speaking kindly and positively to your family. Try to say only positive words:

   - "Walk carefully and slowly," instead of "Don't run."
   - "Remember your appointment," instead of "Don't forget."
   - "I need your help with the groceries," instead of "You're lazy, you never help."

2. Think of your childhood, and of all the names people called you (the labels). Which of these labels have stuck? Make a list and rename yourself in more positive terms.

   - Lazy—Relaxed
   - Slow—Laid back
   - Ugly—Unusual
   - Stubborn—Persistent
   - Hardheaded—Determined

---

3. Think of your spouse, child, or a good friend. Turn all the negative labels to positive ones.

4. For one day, list all the times you say, "No" or "I can't," and all the times you say, "Yes" or "I can." Strive to be an "I can" person.

NOTES

_____
_____
_____
_____
_____
_____
_____
_____
_____
_____
_____
_____
_____
_____
_____
_____
_____
_____
_____

NOTES

HAPPINESS: It's In The Bag!

Chapter 4

A Penny

Money Dynamics

A penny is just a penny, the smallest denomination of our currency. It is worth only $1/100^{th}$ of a dollar. It is such a small unit of exchange that we rarely pay attention to it. Who stops to pick up a penny on the sidewalk anymore? Often, containers of pennies are kept by cash registers and given to customers to help make exact change.

> *To generate prosperity in your own life, you must open your mind to it.*
>
> *— Catherine Ponder*

The penny appears insignificant, but it is a reminder of an important relationship—our relationship with money. As a marriage and family therapist, I am often amazed that my clients will disclose in dramatic detail their most intimate sexual secrets but will rarely talk about their money secrets, concerns, or conflicts.

The relationship with money is such an emotionally volatile issue that it remains too private for many of us to share, even with our therapist (and certainly not with our significant other). This money relationship can be the most hostile and confusing relationship individuals have. The money secrets, buried so deeply inside, begin to grow and control all aspects of our lives.

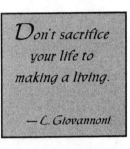

Don't sacrifice your life to making a living.

— C. Giovannoni

People feel controlled by money, but actually we are controlled by fear. Fear blinds us and keeps us from looking openly at our relationship with money. Anything unknown can be fearful and mysterious. If we keep money locked in a deep, secret vault, it will continue to cause pain and to control us.

Money permeates every area of our lives. It represents power, freedom, and security. It defines who we are, where we live, what we do and don't do. It influences our dreams and goals.

We trade the time in our lives for money, so time *is* money. Yet we rarely stop long enough to realize what that means. If I spend eight hours working for $100 and then go out and buy a pair of designer shoes for $90, is that what I am working for? If we are going to trade time for money, let's make sure we value what we spend the money on, just as we value the time it took to earn it.

The penny reminds us to define and evaluate our relationship with money. Take control by learning about your finances. Invest in a money management course, and take a look at how you might balance saving and spending. Be grateful for the prosperity that comes your way.

A penny reminds us to pay attention to our relationship with money. You can have a delightful dance with money if you lead. Enjoy the dance.

ACTIVITIES FOR UNDERSTANDING YOUR MONEY DYNAMICS

1. For one week, write down everything that you spend money on, down to the last penny. (Carry a small notebook with you for accuracy.) What does the week's spending tell you about what you value? At the end of the week, take a sheet of paper and list your expenses in the appropriate categories.

Needs (Basics)	Wants (Desires)	Pure Extravagance
transportation/car	car with all the bells & whistles	chauffeured limousine

   How much life energy did you trade for wants and extravagances? Were they worth the price? (Both figuratively and literally.)

2. Examine the money patterns you learned from your parents—write down the messages they gave you. Now rewrite some messages you'd like to give yourself.

   Example: I will have all the money I need to feel that my life is financially secure. Write the messages you are passing on to your children. (If you don't have children, just pretend you do.)

3. Notice how you react, mentally and physically, when you are in a bank or around wealthy people.

NOTES

_____

_____

_____

_____

_____

_____

_____

_____

_____

_____

_____

_____

_____

_____

_____

_____

_____

HAPPINESS: It's In The Bag!

Chapter 5

A Penny

In God We Trust

One last thought on the penny: *In God We Trust*, written on the penny, is a reminder to trust in God or a higher power. What does it mean to trust God? It means we have faith that there is a larger purpose or order.

Our forefathers founded this nation as a refuge for those who were persecuted for their beliefs. To them, the right to practice the religion one chooses was as vital as life itself. Over the past 200 years, religion has continued to play a major role in America, though it has changed greatly. This is a country with diverse religious and spiritual practices.

Spirituality speaks to the soul, the core or center of each of us. Our values and beliefs govern our existence and our actions. For many, these beliefs are

> *The most beautiful thing we can experience is the mysterious. It is the source of all true art and science.*
>
> — *Albert Einstein*

private; others are more vocal. But almost all of us hold our spiritual notions dear to our hearts.

Some people express their spirituality through prayer, meditation, or the reading of scriptures. For some, art, literature, or music can speak to the soul. Still others find spiritual awakening in their connection to nature or animals. And for some people,

> *The real voyage of discovery consists not in seeking new landscapes but in having new eyes.*
>
> — *Marcel Proust*

> *We are not human beings having a spiritual experience. We are spiritual beings having a human experience.*
>
> — *Teilhard de Chardin*

spirituality can be a combination of any and all of these. The renewal of our spirit through our spirituality refreshes our being and keeps us moving forward. It transforms our daily lives to a more meaningful existence of connection and oneness.

Today, at the turn of the century, we continue to be a society that values spiritual knowledge. One look at the bestseller list in recent years shows a society clamoring for insight into our inner lives, our souls, and even life after death.

The "In God We Trust" inscription on a penny reminds us to trust in a higher power.

ACTIVITIES FOR DEVELOPING
SPIRITUAL INSIGHT

1. Let a circle represent your life. There are four aspects of life to consider: physical, mental, emotional, and spiritual. Divide the circle to show how much time you spend daily in each area. Do you feel comfortable with the division? What would you change? This week, make an effort to spend more time on your spiritual life and notice how it feels.

2. What do you believe regarding reincarnation, life after death, tithing, angels, God, many Gods, the ten commandments, Jesus as our savior, Buddha, Krishna, Mohammed, karma, faith, prayer, meditation, the rosary, and so forth?

3. What role does religion or spirituality play in your life? How do you define your spiritual life? What is your core spiritual belief? How important is it to you? Write a spiritual mission statement. Include any thoughts that are important to you.

4. Notice how your religious and/or spiritual beliefs manifest themselves in your daily life: in how you treat people, for instance, or in your diet, charitable giving, etc. Do you feel any conflicts with your beliefs and your actions or your beliefs and your desires?

Example: I've got a craving for a ham sandwich but that goes against my religion.

5. The next time you're with friends, ask them about their spiritual beliefs. Share who you are spiritually with a friend or family member and describe how your beliefs affect your daily life.

NOTES

_____

_____

_____

_____

_____

_____

_____

_____

_____

_____

_____

_____

_____

_____

_____

_____

_____

_____

A PENNY REMINDS US:

■ To share our thoughts and listen with our ears and heart (a penny for your thoughts);

■ To look at both sides (heads or tails?);

■ To develop an "I can" positive view of life (good luck);

■ To define and evaluate our relationship with money ($);

■ To develop and expand our spiritual insight *(In God We Trust)*.

Please use the following space to describe what a penny symbolizes to you.

_____

_____

_____

_____

_____

_____

_____

SYMBOL TWO

A
Hershey's Kiss

Chapter 6

A Hershey's Kiss
Caring Contact and Connection

The sweetness in this little silver-wrapped chocolate reminds me of many things. The first is the richness of a kiss—the symbol of physical love and intimacy. (Passion is just around the corner in the next chapter.) Physical caring and contact are essential, primal ingredients of a healthy life.

From the beginning of life, when a baby enters the world, we see the importance of touch for survival. Babies who are not routinely touched or fondled don't thrive like those who are. Premature babies in incubators also need to be given ample doses of caring touch. This communication without words is so basic to life from birth to death that we cannot function normally without it.

Unfortunately, our society gives double messages about touching. It's okay to cuddle and caress infants, but we cut off the physical intimacy when the children get older, out of the fearful association of all touch with sexual touch. The early dismissal of touch in our lives and the lives of our children creates a society that is starving for this essential ingredient and looking for ways to feed the hungry skin.

I am often amazed when I see families who were raised without this basic connection. In my Italian-American family we passed out hugs and kisses along with the pasta. It was second nature for me to hug and kiss someone when they arrived at our house. Only when I grew up and went away to college did I learn that not everyone had been so fortunate.

In my counseling practice I have to ask permission to hug some people because they have been abused, and any contact is frightening. We all have physical boundaries, and for some people their three-foot personal boundaries can never be permeated. As a therapist I understand this, but I find it very sad.

> *A friend is, as it were, a second self.*
> — Cicero De Amicitia

Our touch-deprived society is searching for ways to fill the void. The boom in the pet industry is no accident. We have learned to substitute the safe petting of an animal for caressing our children and spouses. In many homes, even houseplants get more touch and communication than do members of the family.

Another way we are filling the "touch void" is with contact sports. Football, hockey, soccer, basketball, and even tag, have become the main modes of play at home. Horseplay, arm wrestling, and slaps on the back and rear end replace hugs and kisses for too many children, especially the boys in our society. (Sports are great, but they shouldn't be the only way our kids get positive physical feedback.)

We live in a society of violence and distorted images of touching. For some, inappropriate touching has become better than no touching at all. We see children from abusive homes acting out or passing on the violence just to feel some skin contact or connection.

Jean and Harry Harlow's famous monkey studies showed that without physical contact, monkeys become angry, frightened, and crazy. We humans are no different. When we are deprived of touch we feel angry, frightened, lost, depressed, despondent, and even abandoned. When we are touched lovingly, our muscles relax, tension is released, inner knots of frustration and isolation dissolve, and we feel connected again. This is a society in which the average age for sexual behavior begins at age 14; healthy touching could help turn that around.

Leo Buscaglia (Dr. Hug) was one of the first ten inductees into the Hershey's Hugs Hall of Fame.

"Have you hugged your kid today?" bumper stickers are a helpful reminder of the importance of physical intimacy in the lives of all of us—the huggers as well as the huggees!

Research on patients in hospitals and nursing homes illustrates the vital need for touch in the healing process. In the early phase of the AIDS epidemic, patients were dying from isolation and lack of physical contact, as well as from the disease. Mother Teresa and Princess Diana were two recent role models who demonstrated the value that touching sick people can have in healing both bodies and souls.

The kiss reminds us of another important connection. Just as physical touching is essential for healthy living, emotional touching is also vital. Emotional touching means sharing yourself, listening with your heart, reaching out and helping your neighbor, and developing empathy for others.

Emotional connection provides families and friends with a special bond. In a society that is so transient, with families separated from one another by hundreds and even thousands of miles, the need for emotional connection with friends is imperative. (Note that touching someone emotionally can take time. Most people don't blurt out their deepest desires or concerns after two minutes.)

We know that elderly people are healthier if they have a purpose. That purpose can simply be an emotional connection with others. Visits from volunteers can often help seniors to keep going, because they look forward to seeing those who love and care about them.

The Hershey Foods Corporation recognized that hugs and kisses go together, so they made a gold-wrapped chocolate and named it "Hugs." The Hershey's kiss reminds us to be generous with our hugs and kisses—both physically and emotionally.

ACTIVITIES FOR CREATING CARING CONTACT AND CONNECTION (HUGS AND KISSES)

1. List ways you can touch others, physically and emotionally. Who is important in your life? Call an old friend and reconnect. Let people know they are dear to you. Tell them—and show them.

2. Volunteer! Find an organization you believe in and get involved. Even an hour a month makes a difference.

3. Circle in ink all the activities listed below that you currently do. Circle in pencil some that you are willing to try in order to increase your intimacy level with others and yourself.

Full body massage   Manicure   Pedicure   Exercise   Swim
Reflexology   Hug   Hand massage   Neck massage   Foot massage
Cuddle with a child   Pet an animal   Facial   Cuddle with your partner
Call a friend   Write a letter to an old or new friend   Hold hands
Make Love   Go to lunch/dinner with a friend   Laugh with someone   Kiss

---

NOTES

HAPPINESS: It's In The Bag!

Chapter 7

A Hershey's Kiss

Passion

We need passion in our lives, and I'm not talking just about sexual passion. Passion indicates a deep, moving connection. This little chocolate kiss symbolizes the intense level of love in our lives. How can we draw this out of ourselves?

As a marriage and family therapist, I often hear at least one partner saying, "I love him, but I'm not in love with him." They have lost "that loving feeling" (The Righteous Brothers, 1965). Of course they have—if you don't use it you lose it. This means that we need to practice intimacy daily, to make it a high priority. There are many ways to maintain and increase the passion in our relationships, but the most important is to keep "doing it."

> *Nothing great in the world has been accomplished without passion.*
>
> — G.W.F. Hegel

As our lives become more complicated—with work, children, and elderly parents—passion and sexual intimacy are often the first things to go. We begin to take their presence for granted.

> *Consider how much more often you suffer from your anger and grief, than from those very things for which you are angry and grieved.*
>
> — *Marcus Aurelius*

One thing that can deaden the kiss in our relationships is anger. Let's go back to those busy, hectic lives of ours. We arrive home, expecting it to be a safe haven. But then we have to cook, clean, do laundry, mow the lawn, run the kids here and there, and so on. We feel taken for granted. We don't take the time to talk, so we stifle our feelings and expect our partner to be a mind reader. But he or she is going through the same thing.

So the anger wall gets built, one brick at a time. Before we know it we are hiding behind it, and any kind of passion is the last kind of connection we want. Anger snuffs out the fire of passion. Only when we deal with the anger, can we reach that feeling expressed by Rodin's sculpture *The Kiss*.

Passion can stir in any area of our lives. Perhaps you love your work and have a great deal of enthusiasm for it. Or maybe it's the weekends you have passion for—you love boating, skiing, rock climbing, or gardening. Whatever your passions, relish them and make time for them.

My father was a good example of someone who relished his passion. He was a musician who loved to play the saxophone. At the age of 45, he was diagnosed with Parkinson's Disease, and although the deterioration was slow, by age 65 he was doing poorly. He had to use a wheelchair and could hardly talk. But every week my mother took him to play in the Fort Lauderdale Big

HAPPINESS: It's In The Bag!

Band. She wheeled him right to his seat, and he played his beloved saxophone. Even though his body betrayed him, his passion lived on and kept him going.

A Hershey's kiss reminds us that passion is a basic ingredient for a healthy life. Passion makes us feel alive. It makes our hearts soar and brings magic to the mundane.

> *Hold fast to dreams, for when dreams die, life is a broken-winged bird that cannot fly.*
>
> — *Langston Hughes*

ACTIVITIES FOR AROUSING
PASSION AND RELEASING ANGER

1. Make a list of 20 things you love to do (your passions). Date the last time you did them. If you aren't doing them, start today! Create new passions: join the choir, take golf or tai chi lessons.

2. Plan a special date with your partner or a friend. Do something you or they love to do.

3. Put on your favorite music and dance! Movement is sensual and creates energized feelings.

4. Anger is passion, too. These activities will help you release pent-up feelings of anger.

   a) Face an empty chair and pretend that the person you're angry with is sitting there. Say everything you'd like to tell them, uncensored. Yell, if you feel like it.

   b) If you're feeling angry, do some intense physical exercise like jumping rope, running, or fast bicycling.

NOTES

_____

_____

_____

_____

_____

_____

_____

_____

_____

_____

_____

_____

_____

_____

_____

_____

_____

NOTES

HAPPINESS: It's In The Bag!

Chapter 8

A Hershey's Kiss
It's What's Inside That Counts

Look at that little Hershey's kiss. When we see the silver-wrapped candy, we realize that, in order to get to the chocolate, we have to peel away the wrapping. What a good reminder of real-life relationships! We often have to peel away the outside layers to get to the core of who we are. When people are too concerned with the shiny outside, they may fail to look inside and discover who they are, or who the other person is. The real "good stuff" is inside, yet if we spend too much time arranging and rearranging the outside, we may not *get* to the inside.

> *There is only one journey, going inside yourself.*
>
> — *Rainer*

> *It is only with the heart that one can see rightly: what is essential is invisible to the eye.*
>
> — *Antoine de Saint Exupery*

There's a wonderful story of a Sufi named Malfi, who had lost his house key. He was crawling around outside looking for his key, when a

> *What lies behind you and what lies before you are tiny matters compared to what lies within you.*
>
> — *Emerson*

friend came by. After helping Malfi to look for a while, his friend asked, "Where did you lose the key?" Malfi replied, "Inside the house." "Then why are we looking for it out here?" "Because there's more light out here," said Malfi.

It's easier to look on the outside than it is to go inside and look at ourselves or others. But the only lasting and important ingredients are on the inside.

Remember: your heart has eyes. So look with your heart, and look with your feelings to uncover the core self.

A Hershey's kiss reminds us that it's what's inside that counts. So unwrap the foil and dig in.

ACTIVITIES FOR
UNWRAPPING THE FOIL

1. Write a personal ad requesting a best friend. Describe the inner qualities you'd like them to have.

2. Describe yourself. List five qualities that are your silver wrapping (outside) and five that represent the sweet chocolate (inside).

3. Call or send a card to a friend, spouse, or child, telling them why you appreciate them. (Describe their inner sweetness.)

4. Draw a picture of your outer, physical self—what people see when they first meet you. Then draw your inner self—what people don't see immediately. Now look at the two pictures, and decide if there's a part of your inner self that you'd like to show others more readily. Here's your opportunity to change.

NOTES

_____

_____

_____

_____

_____

_____

_____

_____

_____

_____

_____

_____

_____

_____

_____

_____

_____

_____

HAPPINESS: It's In The Bag!

NOTES

_____

_____

_____

_____

_____

_____

_____

_____

_____

_____

_____

_____

_____

_____

_____

_____

_____

_____

_____

A HERSHEY'S KISS REMINDS US:

■ To share caring contact and connection (xoxoxoxoxoxoxoxox);

■ To create passion (enjoy the [chocolate] flavor);

■ To look inside ourselves and others (unwrap the foil).

Please use the following space to describe what a Hershey's kiss symbolizes to you.

_____

_____

_____

_____

_____

_____

_____

_____

_____

SYMBOL THREE

An
Elastic
Band

HAPPINESS: It's In The Bag!

Chapter 9

An Elastic Band
Risk

An elastic band is a tiny item, capable of being stretched or expanded. Sometimes it takes only a minor pull for the elastic band to change. At other times we need to really tug to get the band the size we want. Just like an elastic band, we need to stretch ourselves by being open to change and appropriate risk-taking in our lives.

> *And the day came when the risk to remain tight in the bud became more painful than the risk it took to blossom.*
>
> — *Anais Nin*

Often we need some pressure exerted on us before we will risk growing or expanding. In fact, most of the time we would prefer to sit in our easy chair and stay exactly as we are, because many of us are resistant to change.

"There are only two things in life that we can be sure of," according to author Dr. Leo Buscaglia, "death and change, and we don't like either very much." But only when we expand, grow, and take some risks do we increase our awareness and raise our self-esteem. We then find ourselves enjoying new areas of life.

When an elastic band is pulled there's inherent tension. When we have out-side pressure exerted on us to change we may feel tension. (Perhaps you have a baby on the way and you need to change jobs to make ends meet.) It can be difficult learning to live with this tension and finding balance.

> *One can never consent to creep when one feels an impulse to soar.*
>
> *— Helen Keller*

Balance is the key ingredient to risk-taking. We want to embrace change, but we don't want to stretch beyond our capabilities and snap apart like a rubber band.

When I talk about risk, many of my clients assume I'm talking about dangerous physical risks, such as bungee jumping or mountain climbing. Appropriate physical risk might be of interest to you. Perhaps you want to learn to ski; that's great. But risk-taking can also be emotional, intellectual, financial, or spiritual.

An emotional risk might be telling a person for the first time that you love them. An intellectual risk might be taking a class in the philosophy of the ancient Greeks. A spiritual risk could be going to a weekend meditation retreat. A financial risk might be investing in the stock market for the first time or starting your own business.

The type of risk we are inclined to take often varies with our gender and our personality. For example, after a death in the family, a woman is more likely to share her emotions about the loss than is a man. An extrovert is more inclined to talk to strangers than is an introvert.

The process of planned risk-taking, however, is similar for everyone. First, realize that you want to change. Next, make a decision to take an appropriate risk. Third, make a plan, identify alternatives, and consider consequences. Finally, act, and follow through with perseverance.

Expand your comfort zone. Once you take a risk in one area and it's successful, it's easier to take on a challenge in another part of your life.

Once the elastic band stretches, it may look the same, but it never returns to exactly the same size. It is changed forever. We, too, are changed forever every time we take a risk.

The elasticity of the rubber band reminds us to be open and expand into calculated risks.

ACTIVITIES FOR DEVELOPING
APPROPRIATE RISK-TAKING

1. Think of your present life and situation. Can you think of an area where you need to be open to taking a risk? What can you do *today* to expand yourself? Use this four-step process for risk taking:

    <u>Step 1</u> Identify what needs to be changed. Example: I'm going to die on the vine if I stay in this job.

    <u>Step 2</u> Make the decision to take a risk and *write it down*. (I will actively seek and find a better paying job that I enjoy.)

    <u>Step 3</u> Make a plan. (I will send out letters to friends, go to the library and research job opportunities, read the classified ads, take a course on career development.)

    <u>Step 4</u> Act and follow through. Take baby steps. If you run into a wall, continue to take baby steps in a parallel direction.

2. Fill in the chart with six things you love to do. Check the appropriate column to indicate which category of risk is stretched when you participate in the activity.

HAPPINESS: It's In The Bag!

Activity	Physical	Emotional	Intellectual	Spiritual	Financial
■ Tennis	X				
■					
■					
■					
■					
■					

Example: Maybe one of the things you love to do is play tennis, and that's a physical risk for you. (By risk I don't mean dangerous to your health, I mean challenging.) Maybe most of the things you enjoy fall under the physical and intellectual risk categories, so you may need to take more emotional, spiritual, or financial risks.

3. Take a few small risks outside of your priority area. Do one thing differently today. Listen to new music; really listen to the tone and the words. Wear different color clothes, or put on clothes you have never worn together. Go for a walk in a new place. Take the scenic route to work. Talk to the person in the elevator, or the bank or grocery checkout line. Try your hair parted in a different place or wear your hair in a new style. Go to a lecture on something you know nothing about.

NOTES

_____

_____

_____

_____

_____

_____

_____

_____

_____

_____

_____

_____

_____

_____

_____

_____

_____

_____

HAPPINESS: It's In The Bag!

Chapter 10

An Elastic Band

Resiliency

An elastic band is a symbol of our resiliency, our ability to bounce back, to bend and not break. The willow tree bends and sways in a storm, whereas the rigid oak may snap in half if the winds are too strong.

We all stumble in life. The challenge is to pick ourselves up, brush the dirt off, and come out of the fall with only minor injuries.

Obstacles and problems in life often force us to transcend pain and suffering, frustrations or loss, in order to survive, flourish, and reach our goals.

A lot of research has been done on resilient individuals, helping to turn the focus of psychology away from what causes damage to people (a victim model) toward trying to understand what makes them strong (a healthy model).

Psychologist Sybil Wolin, Ph.D., and her husband, psychiatrist Steve Wolin,

> *For a righteous man falls seven times, and rises again.*
>
> — *Proverbs 24:16*

M.D., co-authored the popular book, *The Resilient Self*. The Wolins have identified six qualities of resilient people: insight, humor, independence, initiative, creativity, and morality. In their work, the Wolins encourage individuals to discover their "Survivor's Pride," which means reframing the way they see themselves. People learn to acknowledge their strengths, as well as the coping skills they developed during the rough times.

> *Never give in. never give in. never, never, never...*
>
> —*Winston Churchill*

Other research supports the finding that resilient people share common traits. They all have a basic belief in their ability to set goals and to change. Resilient people recognize their strengths and see themselves as strategists. They have an ability to perceive bad times as temporary and have faith in the future or a higher power. Resilient people do not try to go it alone. Their most important characteristic is the ability to create or expand their circle of support, even if they didn't start out in a loving environment.

One of the most interesting outcomes of this research is that experts now believe that resiliency isn't only innate, but can be learned.

The elasticity of the rubber band reminds us to be flexible and that we can learn to bounce back from a trauma. An elastic band is shaped like a circle that can be expanded. This reminds us to expand our circle of friends and mentors so we can support one another in realizing our dreams.

ACTIVITIES FOR DEVELOPING RESILIENCY

1. Divide the lines below into five-year segments. Jot down a significant event that made you grow during each five-year period. (These can be positive events like a great college experience, or challenging situations like losing a job.) Some time frames may have more than one event. Add as many as you like. When was the most growth-producing time(s) in your life?

   Which of the following resiliency traits did you use during the rough times to bounce back? Insight, humor, creativity, independence, initiative, morality.

   _____

   _____

   _____

2. Think of a situation when you were resilient. Then write which resiliency traits you used to recover.

   Example: (True story) When I was visiting Washington, D.C., my luggage was stolen from my rental car. I had just been to the Holocaust Museum and realized that the inconvenience of being robbed was nothing compared to what happened to the people in the concentration camps (insight). The good news was that I didn't have to get in the luggage line at the airport and I got to buy all new clothes (humor). I temporarily fixed the broken window using borrowed cardboard and masking tape so I could drive the car in the rain (creativity).

3. Edith Grotberg, Ph.D., heads an international resiliency project. The following exercise is based on her work.

   Organize your strengths into three simple categories:

   a) I am. . . .

   b) I have . . . .

   c) I can. . . .

   Example:

   a) I am a person who is kind to others, lives in the present, and loves life.

   b) I have strong role models, great friends, an interesting job, and a loving partner.

   c) I can communicate well, motivate others, and finish projects that I start.

NOTES

_____
_____
_____
_____
_____
_____
_____
_____
_____
_____
_____
_____
_____
_____
_____
_____
_____
_____
_____

NOTES

HAPPINESS: It's In The Bag!

Chapter 11

An Elastic Band
Stretch

The way an elastic band stretches symbolizes the importance of physical motion for a healthy body and mind. Doctors tell us that regular exercise does more than just combat fat and bad cholesterol. It can also lift our mood. We can look at exercise as a first-line treatment for depression.

I used to facilitate a depression support group for our local mental health association. Every week we began the meetings with gentle stretches, reaching for the sky, bending and touching the earth at our toes, and then opening up our diaphragms and chests with arm stretches to our sides.

> *Stimulated by exercise. our life-flame burns with a clearer ray. and we are charged with the joy of being wholly alive.*
>
> — *Gene Tunney*

The participants often joked that the session was more like an exercise class than a depression support group. But they soon began stretching on their own as part of their daily rituals and found that their depression lessened.

Emotional support, stretching, and medication might all be necessary to help cure depression. Drugs may help a disturbed person feel functional, but exercise helps a person feel vibrant.

Doctors are now handing out written prescriptions instructing their patients to start an exercise regime. If you have couch potato tendencies, then exercise regularly with a friend or join a class. Just as an elastic band holds things together, when we have an exercise buddy it helps us to hold our commitment together.

Our society is becoming increasingly technological, and as a result, more sedentary. Yet stretching (exercising) and breathing are essential to keep the brain functioning efficiently. The brain needs one quarter of your body's total fuel supply. It also needs oxygen. You can get a quick boost by yawning a few times or breathing deeply.

My work as a therapist is quite sedentary. I often sit for eight or nine hours a day with only five-minute breaks. This lifestyle caught up with me when I entered menopause. I found myself in one of the deepest depressions I had ever experienced. I was almost immobile. In a desperate attempt to feel better I joined a health club and began to work out. I dragged myself to the club first thing in the morning, got on the treadmill or bike, and began lifting weights and stretching. I'm not going to say that I breezed through menopause, but at least I **breathed** through it with more serenity, lightness, and control.

An elastic band reminds us to stretch, exercise, and breathe for mental and physical health.

ACTIVITIES FOR STRETCHING THE BODY

1. Find a partner and exercise together. This could be a personal trainer, a neighbor, a class, a group of runners, or a dog. Make a plan to exercise for at least 30 minutes, three to four times per week.

2. Start a yoga class. Buy or rent a yoga video; there are many excellent tapes available.

3. Stretch. Stand up and reach for the sky, feel your vertebrae open up, bend forward and let your arms and neck dangle, and relax into the stretch. If you're like me and can't touch your toes, don't strain, just feel the stretch. Bend from side to side.

4. Most people's breathing becomes very shallow or even stops briefly when they are scared or anxious. Take a deep breath in through your nose, hold for the count of five, and slowly blow the breath out through your mouth like you're blowing bubbles. Repeat this three times and you will feel calmer.

5. Yawn deliberately a few times every hour.

NOTES

HAPPINESS: It's In The Bag!

NOTES

_____
_____
_____
_____
_____
_____
_____
_____
_____
_____
_____
_____
_____
_____
_____
_____
_____
_____
_____

AN ELASTIC BAND REMINDS US:

■ To expand our comfort zone (risk);

■ That we can snap back into place (resiliency);

■ To exercise and breathe (stretch).

Please use the following space to describe what an elastic band symbolizes to you.

_____

_____

_____

_____

_____

_____

_____

_____

SYMBOL FOUR

A Pencil

HAPPINESS: It's In The Bag!

Chapter 12

A Pencil

Written Communication

A pencil is a basic tool of written communication, a slender, rod-shaped, wooden instrument with a center of graphite. It is a light, economical, and dependable tool. Pencils work by manual control; the only energy source you need is yourself. There is no need to worry about power surges, or your computer freezing, or accidentally hitting the delete button and losing your work. You are in complete control of the output. The pencil is the middleman for the translation of an idea from thought to written reality.

> *Writing is an exploration. You start from nothing and learn as you go.*
>
> — *E.C. Doctorow*

The pencil helps us to share our thoughts in a more permanent form through writing. We see our words on paper, and they come to life. Writing is a tangible, personal representation of who we are. It is a means of experiencing life and expressing emotions, notions, entertainment, and facts—as well as documenting history. We can be as elaborate or as simple as we choose in sharing our message, just by using a pencil to do the job.

When you first learned to write, you may have received a diary. The diary, or journal, is one of the primary tools I suggest to my clients for helping them to discover their own personal wisdom, actualize their dreams, and release their demons.

Many years ago, I had a deeply troubled family in therapy. Two teenage children were diagnosed with bipolar disorder, there were serious financial problems, and the husband was having an affair. The overprotective mother felt desperate as she watched her family disintegrate and her life spin out of control. She searched for a way to stay connected to her children. Since she loved writing, she used a journal, in which she wrote letters to her daughters and invited them to reply. This mother/daughter journal became a valued treasure. They wrote about their fears, hopes, and dreams—a little of everything. Sometimes they just talked about silly things, crazy conversations, or their favorite foods.

> *Writing is like running, the more you do it, the better you get at it.*
>
> — *Natalie Goldberg*

The journal helped them to weather the storm together. It was a safe haven for learning about themselves and one another. Their dialogue became a precursor to healthy action, and now their relationship is stronger than ever.

I have also seen couples use this technique to improve their relationships. Marriage enrichment programs employ letter-writing to develop (or rekindle) intimacy and emotional connection. Writing increases commitment and says, "This marriage is important and I'm taking the time to write and prove it!"

Writing helps to forge a link between your heart and mind—just what a relationship needs. The permanent nature of the written word helps to clarify the issues between people and to lessen the chance of miscommunication. This is why we have contracts. Writing doesn't have "tone" the way that speaking does. What you see is what you get!

Any and all forms of written communication are vital for healthy relationships. So send letters, postcards, e-mail, faxes, or cards for any reason or occasion. Write it down, drop a line, say, "Hello, just thinking of you," or "Thank you." But say it in writing. It "sounds" louder, and it lasts longer.

When my daughter left for college, I vowed to do something meaningful to stay connected. I bought dozens of postcards and tried to send them daily. Most of them simply said, "Love you, miss you, are you studying?" or "Hang in there." The cards now provide a sweet memoir of her college years, and they strengthened our bond.

One more thing: let's make sure to use the pencil as a tool to help us, not to make our lives more encumbered and stressful. "To do" lists are great for organizing your life, but it's easy to become a slave to them. Too often, I see people who are stressed-out because they feel they will never get everything done. They focus on the things left "to do" on the list, rather than on the positive "I did it!" list. Look often at what you *have accomplished*, not just at what remains to be done.

We all have pencils lying around our home, school, or office. They serve as reminders that the written word is a fundamental form of communication and that the simple pencil is a magnificent tool.

ACTIVITIES FOR ENLIVENING
WRITTEN COMMUNICATION

Note: For all of these activities, please hand-write. We use more motor skills when we write by hand rather than typing, and this accesses our emotions to a greater degree.

1. Start a journal today. Journal writing is an important growth experience. In *The Artist's Way,* Julia Cameron suggests writing three longhand pages every morning as soon as you arise. This pencil-to-paper technique will help you capture the dream state and awaken your creativity. It can also facilitate "brain drain," a sense of just letting out the concern and worries of the day or night.

   Example: "This morning my body aches, it's so hard to move. I know that I need to get to the gym, because only then can I get the blood flowing again. How I hate this feeling! Have to call Kirsten and see if the chair got delivered and if she likes it. Hope it goes in her dorm and fits under the loft. She sounded so sad the last few times we talked. I know it's hard for her to adjust to college and dorm life. Maybe she should have gone closer to home, 12 hours is such a long way away..."

2. Start scripting. Scripting is a tool that helps you create your future with a wishful writing technique that re-trains your unconscious. Write all the dreams and hopes you have as if they were *already happening* (in the present tense). Create your vision in writing. Do this once a month, then set it aside, rereading it weekly and making any updates or changes. Focus on the positive.

   Example: "I am really finding satisfaction in my work. I'm using my creativity and teaching skills to help my clients. The book that I've been working on is flowing along, and I've found more quiet time in which to write. My editor has just found a publisher, and we are in the middle of negotiations. I'm truly enjoying eating healthy foods and working out. My relationship with Kirsten is deepening and we are relating to each other in more subtle ways."

3. Start a two-way, three-way, or family journal.

4. Create an "I did it!" list. At the end of the day, write down everything you accomplished during the day. The "I did it!" list focuses on the positive. We learn self-validation for work accomplished, rather than self-criticism for what remains on the (endless) "To do" list.

NOTES

_____

_____

_____

_____

_____

_____

_____

_____

_____

_____

_____

_____

_____

_____

_____

_____

_____

_____

_____

HAPPINESS: It's In The Bag!

Chapter 13

A Pencil
Emotional Release

Have you ever broken a pencil in two while in a rage? Just snapping the pencil makes you feel better. Researchers have found that writing, not just breaking the pencil, can be a healthy way to release anger because it actually lowers blood pressure! Wouldn't it be great if the drug companies gave out writing journals with their high blood pressure medication?

But why do we have so much pent-up anger? Take a look at babies. They cry, laugh, smile, and move their arms and legs. Infants automatically release feelings through these channels. When we grow up, we learn to censor our expression of emotion, especially those emotions society considers "unpleasant" or "negative." We contain these emotions until the container overflows, and they come bursting out in inappropriate ways.

Feelings aren't negative or positive, it's the expression of them that can be perceived as good or bad for us. There are four primary categories of emotion: mad, sad, glad, and scared. All of them need to be released. But most of us are better at releasing glad or happy feelings than at releasing angry, sad, and fearful ones.

Learning how to deal with anger and to let go of pain are two major problems for society today. One needs only to look at the newspaper or the evening news for proof of that. In addition, anger can accelerate many health problems, such as high blood pressure, ulcers, and cancer. Learning sound ways to release our anger will improve not only our health, but our financial situation as well, because we won't need to visit the doctor as often.

> *Men with clenched fists cannot shake hands.*
>
> — *Sufi Teaching*

Over the years I've watched clients writing letters during therapy to parents, spouses, ex-spouses, children, friends, ex-friends, partners, sexual abusers, and even aborted fetuses. Some clients were in tears during the exercise because the writing evoked horrid memories of trauma. The letters were read aloud to me and then buried, burned, or ripped up and flushed away. Please note: a handwritten blowing-off-steam or releasing-pain letter facilitates the healing process, but should **not** be sent.

Another important use for the pencil is as a method for discussion and problem solving on issues that are too emotionally charged or toxic to talk about. Putting pencil to paper helps us to clarify our ideas and points, making it easier for us to understand ourselves and others. Writing can create a rational form of communication in the heat of a very irrational time.

I teach families to take a "writing timeout." This means they walk away from the person they are in conflict with, grab a pencil, and write down their rage and aggravation. Anger, after all, is only agitated energy. And writing is such a healthy way to release this energy!

But, here's the trick: write, read what you have written, and then set it aside. When you have cooled off, reread it and decide what you want to do with it— bury it, crumple it, save it, burn it, or edit it to be constructive, so you can share it with the person you are in conflict with.

Remember, receiving a letter full of irrational rantings is very unpleasant, and does **not** pave the way to clear communication. Such letters cause hurt feelings, and will put the receiver on the defensive and in "reaction mode," instead of in an open, receptive, and aware state. Use the pencil as a tool to release "negative" painful emotions, but be careful not to inflict them on anyone else. Do it "write."

ACTIVITIES FOR RELEASING EMOTIONS

1. Free associate. Write the word ANGER at the top of the page. Think of all the things you are angry about, or the people you are angry with. Just start writing, and write it all out—no censoring. Let out all the rage and garbage. Then tear up the paper and take it to the trash. Think or visualize that the anger is being released.

   Repeat this activity with SAD and AFRAID.

2. Think of a person who has hurt you and write an apology letter *from* that person to you. Get into the other person's shoes, then write everything you need to hear in order to forgive them. (You know what you need, so say it in writing to yourself.) Read the letter out loud to a friend or to yourself. Let yourself hear it and accept it. Then move on.

3. Write a letter *to* someone who has hurt you. Explain your pain and how their behavior has affected you. Be as specific as possible. <u>Do not mail the letter</u>. Keep it a day or two, reread it, revise it. Then tear it up, burn it, or bury it. Imagine letting go of the pain or rage. If you think of the pain again, remember how you let go of it once, and keep your intent to do so again.

4. As an alternative to arguing with someone, agree to dialogue all toxic ex-

HAPPINESS: It's In The Bag!

changes on paper. Take a "writing timeout" during a conflict, with each of you writing out your thoughts. Then exchange letters and respond. If no agreement can be reached, agree to disagree.

5. Cross out all the feelings below that you're comfortable with. Circle all the feelings that make you uncomfortable. This week, focus on one of the circled words and see if you can feel easier with that emotion. This will help you to identify feelings without judgment.

aggressive   alienated   angry   anxious   confident   curious   depressed
determined   discouraged   embarrassed   enthusiastic   envious   excited
fearful   glad   guilty   helpless   hopeful   hostile   humiliated   lonely
loved   mad   mischievous   optimistic   paranoid   peaceful   proud
regretful   relieved   sad   satisfied   scared   shy   sorry   stubborn
suspicious   undecided   withdrawn

NOTES

_____

_____

_____

_____

_____

_____

_____

_____

_____

_____

_____

_____

_____

_____

_____

_____

_____

_____

_____

Chapter 14

A Pencil

Erase It

A pencil with an eraser on top symbolizes the need to take responsibility for our mistakes, and to mend the mistakes we've made with people by apologizing. We also need to forgive ourselves and others for making mistakes, and then move on. Dwelling on mistakes serves no purpose.

As kids, we often used up the eraser first. We felt free to make use of it and to start over. In fact, we could buy another eraser, pop it on our pencil, and get back to work. Most adults rarely use an eraser. Perhaps this symbolizes our view of mistakes, our inability to admit to them and try again.

> *Write injuries in dust. benefits in marble.*
>
> *— Benjamin Franklin*

"Love means never having to say you're sorry," was a naïve message from the movie *Love Story*. Real life and real love can be messy at times. It is a dangerous illusion to think that true romantic love can continue indefinitely, with no struggle and no conflict. Loving relationships are hard work, and people who live together can drive each other crazy over the trivial matters involved in sharing the same space—let alone the same bed! Close proximity makes us vulnerable. The person closest to us knows us the best and can hurt us the most. And that person may be the one who receives the brunt of our anger, even if they had nothing to do with the rotten day we had at work or school.

> *It is easier to forgive an enemy than to forgive a friend.*
>
> *— William Blake*

It's easy to erase what is written; it takes just a flick of the wrist. And with a little practice, it's easy to say two little words, "I'm sorry," and to ask for forgiveness from others and ourselves. An apology says, "I'm big enough to admit that I was wrong, and I care enough to tell you." An apology opens up the receiver's heart and helps them to forgive you.

Forgiveness is a process made easier with words ("I'm sorry") and actions (changed behavior). Use both, because actions speak as loudly as words.

Being able to forgive is essential for healthy living. Forgiving releases the hurt and anger that have been controlling our lives and thoughts. It is hard work to forgive emotional injuries, and it may take longer than you think. Remember that the willingness to forgive takes courage and strength.

Some things feel too atrocious to forgive. If you feel that you can't forgive yet, or if the person hasn't asked for forgiveness, just allow yourself to be open to the possibility. It will be worth it, because in bestowing the gift of forgiveness, we ourselves are healed and freed from bondage.

A pencil with an eraser reminds us that love means being *able* to say, "I'm sorry," as well as to accept the apologies of others, and to forgive them.

ACTIVITIES FOR PRACTICING "ERASING" MISTAKES AND MOVING ON

1. Is there someone you owe an apology to? Find a card, write a short letter, or make a phone call, and say, "I'm sorry." Be specific about what you are sorry for, and indicate a changed action that you will do from now on.

    Formula for an apology:

    (Name), I'm sorry for (action that offended). I will try to (corrective action).

    Example:

    "John, I'm sorry for calling you an inconsiderate idiot. I won't call you names in the future. If I disagree with the way you're doing things, I'll find a constructive, clear way to communicate my feelings."

2. Look in the mirror and practice saying, "I'm sorry." See how you look. Try it on: say "I'm sorry" to yourself. See how it fits. Be as specific as possible.

3. Make a list of things you need to forgive yourself for. Write yourself an apology. Put it in an envelope and save it. When you feel angry with yourself, take it out and reread it.

Example:

Dear Dianne, I'm sorry for not teaching you how to handle rage and anger. I know you aren't able to express your anger and hope you will learn to state directly what gets you upset, instead of stuffing it down with comfort foods.

Love, Dianne

4. If you are so upset with someone that you can't forgive them yet, try this: every day for the next week visualize that person as being contrite and saying (and meaning), "I'm sorry." Just imagine that they are now worthy of accepting your forgiveness.

5. Say, "I'm sorry," when you make a mistake during the next 28 days. It takes 28 days to change a habit. Make this a new habit.

NOTES

_____

_____

_____

_____

_____

_____

_____

_____

_____

_____

_____

_____

_____

_____

_____

_____

_____

A PENCIL REMINDS US:

■ To share our thoughts and feelings on paper (written communication);

■ To address our feelings and let them go (emotional release);

■ To say that we're sorry and to forgive (erase it).

Please use the following space to describe what a pencil symbolizes to you.

_____

_____

_____

_____

_____

_____

_____

_____

_____

HAPPINESS: It's In The Bag!

<u>SYMBOL FIVE</u>

A Crayon

HAPPINESS: It's In The Bag!

Chapter 15

A Crayon

Play

A crayon reminds us of ourselves in childhood—perhaps kindergarten or first grade—creating our first picture in a coloring book. That happy, carefree child still lives within each of us. A crayon is the symbol that reminds us to play, an activity we often neglect as we age. Playing may seem like a waste of time; yet, without play, life is without color, passion, fun.

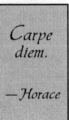

Carpe diem.

— *Horace*

So, as you observe and hold this crayon, think of the times in your life that have been most playful. How do you play? When do you play? Birth order as well as personality impacts our view of play. Some people, especially if they are the youngest in their family, seem to find it easier to play. They are the ones who have crayons or a set of magic markers stashed in a drawer, or who are always telling jokes or playing tricks on others.

I am a firstborn who viewed life very seriously and considered play too frivo-

> *You're only here for a short visit. Don't hurry. Don't worry. And be sure to smell the flowers along the way.*
>
> — *Walter Hagen*

lous an activity for adults. But I knew that play was important for kids, so when my daughter was born I "imported" a good friend—an adult who was the baby in his own family—and he romped with my daughter on the floor, and tossed her up into the air. He knew how to be goofy. I learned from him how to add playfulness to my daughter's life, and how to add it to my own. Now when I go to a restaurant that has crayons and paper tablecloths, I dive right into creating a fantasy drawing. If a string quartet comes to serenade my dinner, I open myself to the fun, instead of wanting to crawl under the table. Most people enjoy dining out, but would not be comfortable drawing on the table or being serenaded. They would rather go to the dentist than be silly.

The crayon reminds us that play isn't frivolous; it is part of a balanced life. Does this area in your life need some attention? Keep the crayon handy, if it does!

HAPPINESS: It's In The Bag!

ACTIVITIES FOR DEVELOPING PLAYFULNESS

1. Below is a list of playful activities. Try one or two of these daily for a month, and notice the change that playing adds to your life.

   Turn on the radio and dance
   Blow bubbles
   Take a bubble bath and play in the water
   Have a water fight
   Blow up balloons
   Jump on a trampoline
   Skip
   Build a model car or airplane
   Make mud pies
   Go to the zoo
   Buy and read a comic book
   Bake cookies and eat them with milk
   Draw a picture and post it on the refrigerator
   Paint your face or nails a wild color
   Read your favorite children's story out loud
   Visit the children's section of a bookstore and sit in a kid's chair and read
   Doodle or make a squiggle on a piece of paper, then create a picture from it
   Print your birth name in large, colorful letters

   Finger-paint
   Play in the rain
   Play jacks
   Hug a tree
   Giggle
   Jump rope
   Color in a coloring book
   Watch cartoons
   Swing on a swing
   Build a sand castle
   Put up a tent and hide inside

2. Add your own ways of playing, and date the last time you played.

NOTES

_____

_____

_____

_____

_____

_____

_____

_____

_____

_____

_____

_____

_____

_____

_____

_____

_____

_____

Chapter 16

A Crayon

Color Your World

Remember the childhood excitement of opening a new box of crayons? The sight and even the smell of the colored wax filled us with glee! It was hard to decide which one to choose first, since every color looked so wonderful. The crayon reminds us that life needs to be bright and beautiful. We must remember to color our world, our lives, our days with beauty.

The crayon takes us back to a time when life was simpler. We didn't worry about bills, or work, or achieving. We simply added color to paper and played. Let's appreciate the color added to our world through nature. We can take the time to notice the blues in the sky, the reds in the sunrises and sunsets, the greens of the leaves, and the browns of the earth. These simple, colorful, basic beauties surround most of us daily, but we rush through our lives, always on a mission. We forget to notice the delicacy, symmetry, and exquisite coloring of roses (not to mention putting on the brakes for 30 seconds and actually smelling them).

Like the orderly color gradation in a box of crayons, our personal environ-

> *Walk on a rainbow trail; walk on a trail of song, and all about you will be beauty. There is a way out of every dark mist, over a rainbow trail.*
>
> — *Edward A. Navajo*

ment needs order too, with things in their proper place. I have worked with numerous couples and families over the years and have noticed an interesting parallel between order and beauty in the home, and order and beauty in the relationship. Couples in therapy who complain of serious relationship problems often talk about the mess in their homes, especially in their bedrooms. They describe disarray and visual disaster areas in their homes, areas which are out of control.

Making our homes more beautiful and ordered is not a luxury, it is a necessity. How can we build healthy relationships in cluttered, dark spaces? We need light, color, and order so we can arrange our lives and breathe life into our relationships. We don't need to spend money to create order and to focus on beauty. Clutter is ugly; simplicity is beautiful. Keep it simple, add color, and maintain order.

While you are adding color to your world, notice the colorful people who are in your life. We need variety in our friendships in order to have rich, exciting lives. Include an array of friends in your life—just like the array of colors in a box of crayons—and they will brighten your days and nights.

The crayon reminds us to create beauty by being "interior" and exterior decorators.

ACTIVITIES FOR COLORING YOUR WORLD

1. Watch the changing colors of a sunrise or sunset.

2. Study the clouds and draw pictures of them.

3. Notice the colors on a bird.

4. Colors are often associated with feelings and energy:

   Red—energized, passionate, emotional
   Blue—sensible, logical
   Pink—loving, warm, affectionate
   Green—healing, emotionally balanced, expansive, abundant
   Orange—communicating well
   Yellow—open to learning, sunny
   Purple—spiritual, royal, wise
   Black—depressed, empty
   Brown—down to earth
   Silver—intuitive, clear
   Gray—confused, cloudy
   White—clear, open, free

Go through the list. Write down a few of the feelings or energies that the colors enliven in you. Does the color of your clothes affect your mood or appearance? Try matching the color you wear to the day's activity.

Example: Wear orange when you have a special request to communicate to your boss or spouse. A tie or scarf with a little orange will do.

5. Look around your home for an area that needs to be ordered and beautified. Start creating beauty today. Buy a plant, or create a backyard or windowsill garden.

6. List the most colorful people in your life. What makes them so bright? Call one of them and make plans for a fun time.

NOTES

NOTES

HAPPINESS: It's In The Bag!

Chapter 17

A Crayon

Creativity

A crayon is one of the first tools children use to express their creativity, and coloring is one of their favorite pastimes. When we are young we learn to explore the world of color and beauty with a crayon. Coloring transports us to another place—the playground of the creative mind.

Usually, kids feel freer to be creative than do adults. Coloring was fun and uninhibited until we learned there was a "right way" to color. The person who thought they would help us to color "correctly" by telling us to stay inside the lines was actually our first critic. Why can't grass be purple? And who says you have to stay inside the lines?

> *I*magination is more important than knowledge.
>
> — *Albert Einstein*

Creativity is looking at an object or concept and seeing it differently than others do, or inventing something (the light bulb). A creative person turns problems into challenges and opportunities.

In what ways are you creative? Is your work a creative outlet? What about the way you organize your day, your desk, or your home? All of these can be areas of creative expression. Your clothing, cars, possessions, artwork, hobbies, and the way you live your life are also creative expressions.

We can also be creative in our problem-solving techniques. I have many drawing materials in my office, but I find that crayons are the most popular. I often use a three-picture drawing technique that I learned from psychotherapist and hypnotist Joyce Mills. I will ask clients to draw a picture of how the problem looks now; this is picture #1. Picture #2 is how the problem will look when it's "all better." Picture #3 represents what will help the client to get from picture #1 to picture # 2.

> *Creativity involves breaking out of established patterns in order to look at things in a different way.*
>
> — *Edward DeBono*

Young children under the age of five are eager to do this. They draw powerful pictures because they feel and see solutions to their problems. However, most adults whine and fight doing this exercise. They say, "I can't draw" or "I'm not artistic." That early critic controls their ability to try something different and playful.

This exercise activates the left side of the brain, which defines the problem, and engages the nonverbal right side of the brain through drawing. It unlocks a whole new dimension and provides amazing results, if you're willing to try.

Corporate America has experimented with creative ways to solve problems. A few years ago I read an article in *Bottom Line* magazine that described an innovative technique. When one corporation was faced with a problem, all of its managers sat around a table, with each person given a different color baseball

HAPPINESS: It's In The Bag!

cap to wear. The green hat was expected to be the creative thinker and generate lots of ideas. The white hat was the objective thinker and concentrated on the facts. The red hat expressed the emotions, hunches, and intuitive feelings. The black hat was the cautious, negative, doom and gloom, worst-case perspective. The blue hat gave the objective overview of the entire problem. Something as simple and playful as colored baseball caps generated unorthodox solutions to a complex problem.

Remember to get out your crayons and let your inner child create green cows and pink cats. It takes courage to be creative and color outside the lines of life, but it's worth it!

ACTIVITIES FOR DEVELOPING CREATIVITY

1. The "Switch Hands" technique.

   a)   Spend two minutes making as long a list as you can of the uses for an ordinary pencil. Now switch to your non-dominant hand and continue the list. You will come up with very different uses for the pencil, because this activity activates both sides of the brain.

   b)   Write down one of your problems and list some possible solutions. Now switch hands and continue your solution list. This will generate whole-brain problem solving.

2. If you want to be more creative, you need to spend time with creative people. Contact your local artists' guild and attend meetings or openings. Call some of your most creative friends and go to lunch. Listen to them and notice how they think, dress, behave.

3. Use Joyce Mills' three-picture drawing technique. Think of a problem. Draw how the problem looks now. Label that picture #1. Draw how it will look when it's "all better" and label that picture #2. Then draw picture #3, which is what is needed to get from picture #1 to picture #2. Post your pictures and experience the change.

4. When faced with a problem or challenge, try this creative problem-solving technique. Put a paper and pencil next to your bed. Before you go to sleep, try to define the problem out loud. Then write it down, reviewing all aspects. Repeat the problem before closing your eyes. Three things could happen:

   a) Eureka! You will solve the problem in your sleep.

   b) You will think of a solution in the next few days.

   c) You will not be able to sleep. (Two out of three isn't bad.)

5. Think of any problem. Open a book and point to any word. Think of how you could use the word in solving your problem. This helps you to break out of the darkness of the problem and into more creative light.

6. If you have a complex problem at home or at work, try the colored baseball cap technique. Have each friend or family member wear a different color hat, and ask them to stick to their roles. After every person has had a chance to speak freely without being interrupted, the group discusses the problem and comes up with a solution.

NOTES

_____

_____

_____

_____

_____

_____

_____

_____

_____

_____

_____

_____

_____

_____

_____

_____

HAPPINESS: It's In The Bag!

NOTES

_____

_____

_____

_____

_____

_____

_____

_____

_____

_____

_____

_____

_____

_____

_____

_____

_____

_____

_____

A CRAYON REMINDS US:

■ That it's important to be childlike (play);

■ To find beauty around us—to be an interior and exterior decorator (color your world);

■ To color outside the lines (creativity).

Please use the following space to describe what a crayon symbolizes to you.

_____

_____

_____

_____

_____

_____

_____

_____

HAPPINESS: It's In The Bag!

SYMBOL SIX

A Candle

HAPPINESS: It's In The Bag!

Chapter 18

A Candle

Keep It Light

A candle transforms darkness into light. A candle is a reminder to keep life light with laughter and humor.

When I was a high school counselor in the 1970s and 1980s, I had a sign on my office door that read: "Humor—never leave home without it." During that time I finished my degree as an educational specialist in marriage and family therapy. My work with families helped me realize that I needed a second sign: "Humor—never be home without it."

> *When humor goes, there goes civilization.*
>
> *— Erma Bombeck*

Today we are aware of the positive effect that humor has on our lives and on our health, both mental and physical. We know that children laugh 400 times a day and adults laugh only 15 times a day. *Laughing Matters* magazine reports that laughing 100 times a day is the cardiovascular equivalent of 10 minutes of rowing.

In the 1970s, research was conducted on hospitalized cancer patients who were receiving heavy doses of morphine every few hours. When these patients were shown *I Love Lucy* reruns at medication time, it was found that their scheduled medications could be delayed by one hour, because laughter had increased their ability to tolerate pain.

At many hospitals a "humor cart" has become part of the pain management program. The cart holds funny videos, games, and books—all provided to help patients to laugh, release endorphins, and shift their focus away from pain.

When my daughter Kirsten was three years old, we had an eye-opening experience. We were running to our van after many hours outside in the cold New Jersey winter. As we entered the van, our heads collided; we hit each other very hard. She started to cry and I was blinking back tears. I tried to distract us from our pain.

Since we were blinking, I mentioned that I could only wink my left eye, not my right. Kirsten said she could only wink with her left eye as well. (Some genetic anomaly, I'm sure.) So, through her tears, she tried to wink her right eye. So did I. We made strange, distorted faces as we struggled to wink. After a few minutes, we were both laughing hysterically. Kirsten looked up through her tears and laughter and said, "You know Mommy, when you laugh, nothing hurts."

A candle reminds us to brighten our day with lightness and laughter. So start laughing—or at the very least, try smiling—and find the humor in daily life. Release those endorphins and have some fun.

> *Angels can fly because they take themselves lightly.*
> — G.K. Chesterton

ACTIVITIES FOR KEEPING IT LIGHT

1. Rent and watch some funny videos. Old classic comedy is wonderful; look for *The Three Stooges, I Love Lucy*, and *Abbot and Costello*.

2. Read the comics in the newspaper. Buy a joke book and read it, or just browse the humor section of the bookstore. Find something that makes you laugh.

3. Post or frame your favorite cartoon.

4. Smile at people: at the person in the grocery store, at the person who cuts you off in traffic. Imagine that it is National Smile Day and just smile all day. Notice how it makes you and others feel.

5. Who are the funniest people you know? Make a laugh list with names and phone numbers. When you need a laugh, call a friend on the list. Thank them for the gift of laughter, humor, and lightness in your life.

6. Mail your friend a funny comic or joke. Make someone laugh. Laughter is contagious. Pass it on.

NOTES

_____

_____

_____

_____

_____

_____

_____

_____

_____

_____

_____

_____

_____

_____

_____

_____

_____

_____

_____

_____

Chapter 19

A Candle

Ritual

A birthday candle heralds another year of life. The birthday ritual originated in Germany. One candle was placed on the cake for each year and one candle for growth. When the candles were blown out, a wish was made, and the smoke carried the wish to God.

The birthday celebration ritual helps us to focus on the future, while reminding us of our connection with the past. The word "ritual" comes from the Latin word *ritus*, or river, which is symbolic of the life force that flows through all living things. Rituals increase balance and connection with ourselves, with others, and with the larger world.

> *Rituals are not the path, they are the reminder that there is a path.*
>
> — *Emmanuel*

Rituals—repeated ceremonial acts—are integral parts of nature and of our daily lives. They can be conscious or unconscious actions, usually involving some art form, which help to deepen our experience. From birth to death, our lives are shaped by ritualistic behaviors.

You can probably think of many daily habits you do ritualistically, like drinking your morning cup of coffee, reading the newspaper, brushing your teeth, or checking your e-mail or phone messages as soon as you arrive home. These habits become rituals when we consciously think of the action we are performing. We then allow this action to create a sense of safety, security, and order in our day.

> *Ceremony and ritual spring from our heart of hearts: those who govern us know it well, for they would sooner deny us bread than dare alter the observance of tradition.*
>
> —*F. Gonzalez-Crussi*

In fact, think of what happens when these rituals are missed. Do you feel out of it if you have to rush and miss your morning ritual? Or is rushing part of the morning ritual?

In addition to the daily rituals, ceremonies are often performed at transition times: beginning (birth and promotions), ending (death), merging (marriage and partnership), cycles (birthdays and anniversaries).

As our society has grown and aged, we have failed to keep our rituals current with society's needs. We have many transition times that lack rituals, yet badly need them. American society is in need of a transition ritual from adolescence to adulthood—a rite of passage. We are one of the few cultures lacking this ritual, and we are faced with serious problems because of it. Teenagers create their own rituals for meaning, social connection, and tradition. They may pierce and tattoo body parts, or assume their own style of dress. Gangs form because kids want to feel that they are a part of something, even if it's destructive.

But without a ceremony, or some form of encouragement to move out of these behaviors, people can get stuck in adolescence and wreak havoc on society. In ancient civilizations, a boy went into the woods to be initiated into manhood by his elders. Ceremonies were held for girls to acknowledge their passage into womanhood when they started menstruating.

Adults lack rituals, too. We need to acknowledge transition times, such as retirement and divorce. Rituals help us realize that generations before us have had the same experience, that we are not isolated, and that other people's experience can help guide us through the transition.

The candle symbolizes the value of ceremonial acts. It reminds us to stop, think, and appreciate a ritual. Be conscious of your habits and transform them into rituals.

ACTIVITIES FOR ENHANCING
YOUR LIFE THROUGH RITUALS

1. Think of three daily rituals that you do almost unconsciously. Make them conscious. Be aware of their importance in your day. Appreciate the ritual for the comfort it adds to your life.

2. Add a new beginning ritual to your day. For example, you could read an inspirational quote to start your morning in a positive, focused way.

3. Look at your closing rituals for the day. Do you have a bedtime ritual? Children need bedtime rituals, and so do adults. You could say a prayer of thanks for what you received that day: nourishing food, good health, love, the beauty of nature, etc.

4. Create rituals where they are lacking. If you earn a promotion, honor your achievement with a celebration. Give an award to a parent for outstanding love and guidance. Our society doesn't have a ritual for divorce (ending ritual) other than the issuing of a certificate. It's no wonder that many couples

HAPPINESS: It's In The Bag!

have trouble with closure. Perhaps we could have a few close friends and family members witness a ceremony that acknowledges the dissolution of the marriage.

5. Review holiday rituals. Decide what fits and what needs to be altered. Are your rituals rich with meaning or hollow vestiges of ceremonies?

NOTES

HAPPINESS: It's In The Bag!

Chapter 20

A Candle
Aging Gracefully

When we were children we couldn't wait for our birthday celebration. But somewhere along the way we began to dread birthdays, because they remind us that we are getting older.

The candle reminds us that aging is inevitable, but that doesn't make it bad. In a society that worships youth, it's difficult to realize that we have value and get better with age. Somehow we must educate society about the positive aspects of aging. Our appearance changes with age, but that doesn't mean it's less beautiful. Just as we can appreciate a fine aged wine, we need to learn to honor our vintage bodies and Solomonic wisdom.

> *The greatest thing about getting old is that you don't lose all the other ages you've been.*
>
> —Madeleine L'Engle

The candle symbolizes celebrating and honoring each passing year. The challenge is how to validate and glorify every age by creating new realities. For example, how can we make the 40s carefree, fun, and exciting—reminiscent of those childhood days? How do we incorporate the risk-taking, adventuresome spirit, and dare-to-be-different attitude of adolescence into our 60s?

The first group of Baby Boomers is already over 50 years of age, and the rest are fast approaching the second half of life. They are demanding that the old myths of aging be debunked. It used to be an anomaly to see someone in their late 50s starting a new business, climbing Mt. Fuji, or finishing their college degree. Now we all know such active, inspired people.

> *The joys of my life have nothing to do with age. They do not change. Flowers, the morning and evening light, music, poetry, silence, the goldfinches darting about...*
>
> —*May Sarton*

"Grow old along with me, the best is yet to be" is a wonderful motto for aging gracefully. This Robert Browning quote reminds us to find and become role models for all of life's cycles, and even to actually look forward to aging. Let's choose to make peace with our past, our bodies, and ourselves in order to focus on the best that "is yet to be."

Older people exude a certain knowingness that is attained by decades of experience. Perhaps we can learn from Asian and Native American cultures to value the wisdom of elders. These cultures know that to age gracefully, we must incorporate solitude into our lives. Let's give ourselves the gift of silence, by creating a quiet space, by taking the time to reflect, to meditate, to connect with nature and with our God.

The candle reminds us that we can walk (or run) gracefully into the cycles of aging; there is no need for kicking and screaming.

ACTIVITIES FOR AGING GRACEFULLY

1. Interview someone who is five or ten years your senior. Ask them about their life in recent years. What have they learned and experienced about themselves and their bodies? Ask them to focus on the positive.

2. Write a title for each decade of your life using a song, book, or movie title.

   Example:

   The 20s, *Love Story*; the 30s, *A League of Her Own;* the 40s, *How Dianne Got Her Groove Back;* etc. Write some titles for future decades.

3. Use the scripting technique (refer to the Chapter 12 Activities for Enlivening Written Communication) and create a script for the way you'd like your next few decades to look.

4. Find role models or mentors in people you admire who are aging gracefully. These could be famous people, like Katharine Hepburn, or people you know.

a) Post pictures of them.

b) Spend time with these role models or mentors, if possible. Listen to their stories, share memories and dreams.

5. Have coffee and chat with an elderly neighbor or someone in a retirement community or nursing home.

NOTES

_____
_____
_____
_____
_____
_____
_____
_____
_____
_____
_____
_____
_____
_____
_____
_____
_____
_____
_____

A CANDLE REMINDS US:

■ That when you laugh, nothing hurts (keep it light);

■ To value ceremonial acts (ritual);

■ To grow old along with me, the best is yet to be (aging gracefully).

Please use the following space to describe what a candle symbolizes to you.

_____

_____

_____

_____

_____

_____

_____

_____

_____

SYMBOL SEVEN

A Seashell

Chapter 21

A Seashell
Protection

When I first began giving my "It's in the Bag" lecture, one of the symbols was a seashell, something very plentiful here in Naples, Florida. Seashells can be found in almost every home, and I keep a large vase of them in my counselling office.

When clients are new or have experienced a particularly difficult or painful session, I present them with a seashell. I tell them the story of hermit crabs, who live on the ocean floor. These crabs have a hard skin except for the abdomen, which is soft. In order to protect their soft spot they find a shell and make it their home. The shell is never a perfect fit, and as they grow they need to shed their old shell and find a new one. When a hermit crab is threatened, it withdraws into its shell until the danger has passed.

> *When you come to a roadblock, take a detour.*
>
> —*Mary Kay Ash*

The hermit crab's journey is symbolic of our life journey. We live in the open sea of life, which can be frightening as well as exciting. At transition times, (e.g., when relationships end, or health suffers, or we lose a job, or our child has a crisis) our hard skin may not be hard enough. We feel that our soft belly is exposed, making us vulnerable, and so we seek a shell for safety. We pull the covers up and hide for a while. When it's safe, we come out and try again. This process happens over and over again during our lives.

In fact, every 24 hours is a new journey. The shell reminds us of the importance of going within for a rest or a sound sleep. Our bodies need sleep in order to face another day with alertness and fresh anticipation. If we are in a particularly stressful situation, it's wise to put our feet up periodically and take some additional rest to let the mind and body process the situation and recover. Research shows that napping increases productivity. Different people need different amounts of sleep, and it is vital to respect our own and others' body types and rest requirements.

A seashell symbolizes surviving and growing in the open sea of life by honoring our vulnerability.

ACTIVITIES FOR CREATING PROTECTION

1. When have you been the most vulnerable? Look at the healthy ways you protected yourself (your shell), e.g., by gathering a support system of good friends. Be aware that it's okay to have vulnerable times and to hide out for a while until you get stronger. It's also okay to keep yourself out of harm's way. (If you have an addiction, don't hang out at "the bar.")

2. This week, observe the ways you rest (rest includes not just sleeping, but napping, meditating, and reclining). Make adjustments if you frequently feel fatigued.

3. Think of three times that you had to let go of an old shell (a move, divorce, death, marriage). Rate how vulnerable you felt on a scale of one to five (five being most vulnerable). What new shell did you find to replace the old? (new-found freedom, patience, unconditional love)

NOTES

_____

_____

_____

_____

_____

_____

_____

_____

_____

_____

_____

_____

_____

_____

_____

_____

Chapter 22

A Seashell

One of a Kind

When I walk on the beach, I am struck by the diversity and uniqueness of the shells. Seashells come in so many sizes, styles, and colors. There are billions of them on the beach, but no two are alike. Often it's the small shells that catch our attention, and we can spend hours collecting them. At other times we may opt only for one large conch with a shiny pink interior. It sometimes seems easier to see uniqueness in seashells than in ourselves.

Our high-tech society thrives on mass production, which can make uniqueness and diversity difficult qualities to maintain. We want to have what others have, yet we want it to be uniquely our own (a designer shirt in a rare color). Paradoxically, we want to belong and yet we want to be different. We are constantly striving to find the balance between sameness and uniqueness—two vital ingredients for healthy self-esteem.

When we look at the beach from a distance, we see an exquisite expanse of sand and shells. On closer inspection, we see that while some shells are perfect, many are broken, chipped, or worn down. But they all contribute to making a beautiful beach.

The following story illustrates how everyone has a role to play, flaws and all. There was a water bearer in India who carried two large pots on the end of a pole. He went daily to the stream and returned to his master's house with water. One of the pots was perfect, while the other had a crack, leaking at least half of its contents before the servant reached his master's home. After a year, the perfect pot was proud of its accomplishment. However, the cracked pot was ashamed of its flaw and apologized for its inability to provide a full pot of water at the end of each day's journey. The water bearer told the cracked pot to notice the road as they returned from the stream. The cracked pot watched and saw a wide variety of beautiful flowers blooming only on one side of the road. The water bearer said, "I have always known about your flaw so I took advantage of it. I planted flower seeds on your side of the road, and every day you watered them. If you hadn't been just the way you are, I wouldn't have been able to pick those beautiful flowers to grace my master's table."

> *Two roads diverged in a wood, and I —I took the one less traveled by, and that has made all the difference.*
>
> —*Robert Frost*

Each of us has our own strengths and flaws, just like the pots or the seashells on the beach. Uniqueness is not perfection, but rather specialness; it's what sets us apart from others. Our gift might be that we can make others laugh or that we live our life with integrity. The seashell reminds us that we are each one of a kind and can celebrate our unique qualities.

ACTIVITIES FOR CELEBRATING
YOUR UNIQUE QUALITIES

1. Where do you shine? Make a list of your special talents or gifts and post it on the mirror. How are you using them in your life?

2. Every day for the next week, give thanks for your gifts and talents.

3. Write a thank-you note to yourself for who you are and what you do that is special.

4. Do you have a unique style? Look at your wardrobe, your home, or office/workspace. Do you have a special color that predominates, or certain collections, or a special flair?

5. If you had three other lives to live, who would you be? Are you incorporating any of those talents in your life now? Could you? For example:

Dream	I Could
Actress	Join a local theater group
Singer	Take singing lessons
Author	Write in my journal daily

6. Draw a picture of your uniqueness.

7. Create a personal uniqueness alphabet. For example:

A—Artistic

B—Balanced

C—Creative

NOTES

_____

_____

_____

_____

_____

_____

_____

_____

_____

_____

_____

_____

_____

_____

_____

_____

_____

_____

NOTES

_____

_____

_____

_____

_____

_____

_____

_____

_____

_____

_____

_____

_____

_____

_____

_____

_____

Chapter 23

A Seashell

Mother Nature

> This we know—the Earth does not belong to man—man belongs to the Earth. All things are connected like the blood which unites one family. Whatever befalls the Earth befalls the sons of the Earth. Man did not weave the web of life. He is merely a strand of it. Whatever he does to the web he does to himself.
>
> —*Chief Seattle*

The seashell reminds us that we live in an interconnected web of life. We are not isolated from nature or from one another. Throw a pebble or shell into a pond and watch how the whole pond is affected by the ripples from one small object. In our consumer-driven, information-based culture, we often forget the importance of our relationship to the natural environment.

Ancient cultures revered Mother Nature. They observed her power, not only in the sea, but in the earth, the air, and fire as well. Most of the indigenous peoples of the earth continue to respect nature, and walking in harmony with the earth is an integral part of their teachings.

> *The clearest way into the Universe is through a forest wilderness.*
>
> — *John Muir*

It took our modern American culture until 1970 (the first National Earth Day) to formally honor and celebrate protecting the earth. There is so much we could learn about being stewards of the earth from the Native American and other cultures. Let's honor Mother Nature <u>every</u> day, not only by preserving the environment, but also by enjoying the outdoors.

I wrote much of this book at the beach while listening to the call of the seagulls and the lapping of the waves against the shore. My thinking expands with the warmth of the sun. While you may not have the opportunity to sit at a beach, you can still leave your everyday world of concrete and mortar to spend some time in nature. Even in Manhattan you can visit Central Park and experience the wind blowing through the trees or feel the mist coming off a pond.

The next time you're having a bad day, take a walk in nature and touch the earth with your feet. Notice your surroundings. As you connect with nature you will feel better. Being in nature helps us to get out of the swirling problems in our minds and back into the enjoyment of simple, sensory pleasures—back to living in the present moment.

Without the gifts of the earth we cannot survive. By appreciating and preserving these gifts, we will thrive for generations to come. A seashell reminds us to nourish our relationship with Mother Nature.

HAPPINESS: It's In The Bag!

ACTIVITIES FOR CONNECTING TO MOTHER NATURE

1. Take a nature walk. Be present and experience your surroundings. Finetune your senses; <u>feel</u> the wind, <u>breathe</u> in the smells, <u>hear</u> the sounds, <u>see</u> the colors.

2. Touch the earth today. Collect some small items from nature: a leaf, a shell, driftwood, a flower. Keep them nearby as reminders of your connection with the earth.

3. Start the day off with a silent salute to Mother Nature.

4. Do two or three deeds this week for the earth. Pick up litter, donate your time or money to an environmental organization, recycle, plant a tree.

NOTES

_____

_____

_____

_____

_____

_____

_____

_____

_____

_____

_____

_____

_____

_____

_____

_____

_____

_____

_____

_____

NOTES

_____

_____

_____

_____

_____

_____

_____

_____

_____

_____

_____

_____

_____

_____

_____

_____

_____

_____

A SEASHELL REMINDS US:

■ To honor our vulnerability (protection);

■ To see our uniqueness and diversity (one of a kind);

■ To stay connected with earth, sea, and sky (Mother Nature).

Please use the following space to describe what a seashell symbolizes to you.

_____

_____

_____

_____

_____

_____

_____

_____

_____

CLOSING

Your Lunch Bag to Go

HAPPINESS: It's In The Bag!

Chapter 24

Your Lunch Bag
to Go

HAPPINESS: It's In The Bag! has been an adventure in creative symbolism. Its light and simple format is meant to help clarify your life's priorities and values.

In order to make this "Your Bag," it's time for you to look at your life and see if there are any missing ingredients. If so, what symbol could you cook up for the quality you need to enhance?

A few suggestions:

- ■ a feather for lightness or quietness;
- ■ a rose for more beauty or delicacy;
- ■ a paper clip to hold it all together;
- ■ a band-aid to cover and heal the wounds;
- ■ or a pair of ruby slippers to help you return home.

It's up to you to finish the chapter. Go wild!

In the back of this book, you will find perforated sheets that you can cut apart into illustrated cards representing all of the symbols, as well as several blank cards that you can use to create your own symbols. You will also find some suggestions for using the cards.

Life is full of symbols to help me see,
How to learn, to grow, and just be me.
When I forget to look within
And all my feelings are in a spin,
This bag of symbols takes me where
I learn to handle me with care.

—DD & Friends

We'd love to hear about your personal meaning for these symbols as well as any other symbols that enrich your life. Please send your ideas and insights to:

Dianne Durante, Ed.S., Director
Anchor Counseling and Training Center
812 Anchor Rode Drive
Naples, FL 34103

Email to: **itsinthbag@aol.com**

Or call us at **1-800-545-5801**

or **941-262-6911**

Suggestions for Using the Reminder Cards

1. Shuffle the cards.
2. Draw a card at random and notice any synchronicity.
3. Think of how the symbol is a helpful reminder in your life.

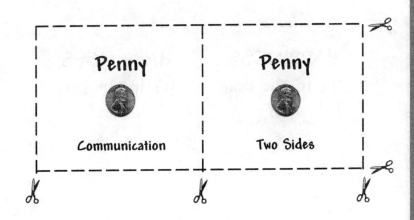

HAPPINESS:
It's In The Bag!

HAPPINESS:
It's In The Bag!

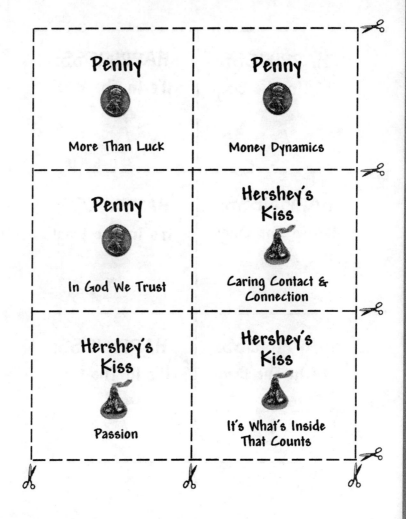

Penny	**Penny**
More Than Luck	Money Dynamics
Penny	**Hershey's Kiss**
In God We Trust	Caring Contact & Connection
Hershey's Kiss	**Hershey's Kiss**
Passion	It's What's Inside That Counts

Elastic Band	Elastic Band
Risk	Resiliency

Elastic Band	Pencil
Stretch	Written Communication

Pencil	Pencil
Emotional Release	Erase It

HAPPINESS:
It's In The Bag!

HAPPINESS:
It's In The Bag!

HAPPINESS:
It's In The Bag!

HAPPINESS:
It's In The Bag!

HAPPINESS:
It's In The Bag!

HAPPINESS:
It's In The Bag!

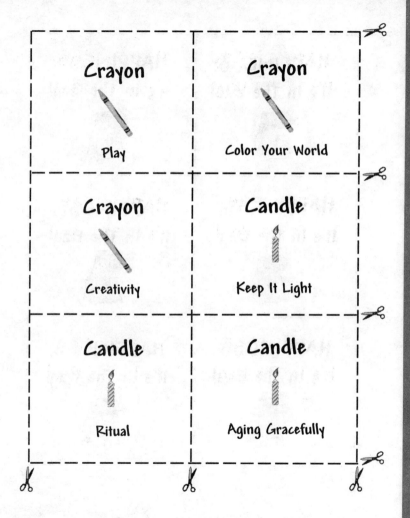

Crayon	Crayon
Play	Color Your World
Crayon	Candle
Creativity	Keep It Light
Candle	Candle
Ritual	Aging Gracefully

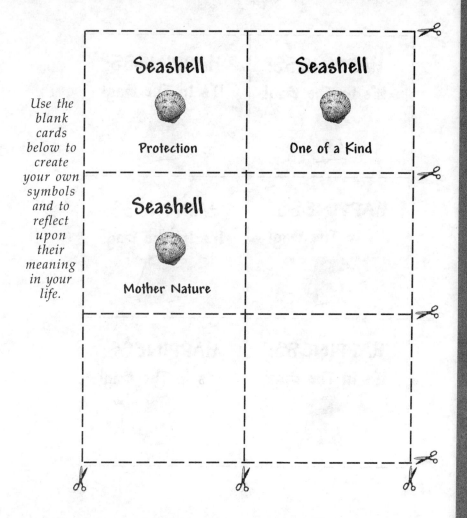

Use the blank cards below to create your own symbols and to reflect upon their meaning in your life.

Seashell

Protection

Seashell

One of a Kind

Seashell

Mother Nature

About the Author

Dianne Durante, Ed.S., is an expert on marriage, family, and the educational system. She has more than 30 years experience as a therapist and educator, has hosted her own radio talk show, and is the author of numerous grants and articles. Dianne is known for her innovative, interactive presentations, which combine symbols and stories to keep audiences laughing as they learn and remember the basics for living a happy life.

She has created and conducted parent education programs for the traditional and blended family, as well as support groups for divorced parents and children of divorce. She has taught psychology and sociology courses at the university level on topics such as women, aging, death, and love.

Dianne completed her Ed.S. in Marriage and Family Therapy at Seton Hall University in South Orange, N.J. She earned her M.Ed. in Counseling Education at William Paterson College in Wayne, N.J., and her B.S. in Education/Psychology from the University of Dayton in Ohio. She has received advanced training in Women, Family Systems, and Alcohol Studies from Rutgers/UMD New Jersey, in addition to training in Ericksonian Hypnosis and NeuroLinguistic Programming. She is a clinical member of the American Association of Marriage and Family Therapists and the American Orthopsychiatric Association.

Born and raised in Chicago, Dianne moved to the New York/New Jersey area to bloom and now flourishes in the sunshine in Naples, Florida. She loves the beach, the color purple, her work, and her family.

* * *

Lane Hawley Cole is a freelance writer when she is not running, biking, rollerblading, or playing golf or tennis.

Quick Order Form

Fax orders: 1-941-403-0548

Telephone orders: Call 1-800-545-5801 or 1-941-262-6911. Have your credit card handy.

Email orders: Itsinthbag.aol.com

Postal orders: Anchor Counseling and Training Center, 812 Anchor Rode Drive, Naples, FL 34103

Please send the following books/journals. I understand that I may return any of them for a full refund—for any reason, no questions asked.

_____

_____

_____

Please send more FREE information on:

❑ Other books/journals   ❑ Speaking/Seminars   ❑ Videos/Cassettes   ❑ Consulting

Name: _____

Address: _____

City: _____ State: _____ Zip: _____

Telephone: _____ Fax: _____

Email Address: _____

Sales Tax: Please add 6% for products shipped to Florida addresses.

Shipping by air: U.S.: $4 for first book and $2 for each additional product. International: $9 for first book; $5 for each additional product (estimate).

Payment: ❑ Cheque   ❑ Credit Card:

❑ Visa   ❑ MasterCard   ❑ Discover

Card number: _____

Name on card: _____ Exp. date: _____/_____